ISBN 978-0-615-36548-0

ABS & ARMS

by

David Kirsch

Illustration by

Steve Wacksman

I'm David Kirsch

and I work with some of the most beautiful people in the world.

Many of my clients regularly have red carpet events on the calendar or the paparazzi stalking their beach vacations, looking for the slightest hint of a paunch or a jiggle. So in my twenty years of training, I've developed some pretty foolproof techniques for toning arms and smoothing abs. These techniques work for celebrities, yes, and they work for the rest of us, too!

Does the bottom of your arm jiggle when you wave goodbye? Are you wearing sweater sets in July, just to keep it covered? Is getting your jeans zipped up in the morning the closest you get to a cardiovascular workout? Are you still calling it baby weight, even though your "baby" just graduated from college?

Guys, this is for you, too! Do you get sand kicked in your face at the beach? Has gym class-dread crept into your adult life? Do you wish you had a six pack and a major set of guns? (I don't mean water guns, and I don't mean cans of Bud.)

I want you to look down, and be honest about whether or not you've got a clear view of all ten toes, and don't tell me that untucked shirt is a fashion statement...I can get you from spare tire to six pack.

I wasn't always as fit as I am today, but I was inspired by Brad Pitt in Thelma and Louise—he was only on screen for a few quick minutes, but it was a sensation. A star was born. You've probably got your moment—maybe it was an Abercrombie and Fitch billboard, maybe it was an old Arnold Schwarzenegger film. Well, here's the thing: It is possible. That can be you. I say this with total confidence, I say this with the weight of experience. Trust me, follow me, and don't even think about cheating. Put down the chips, quit it with the beer, the chocolate, the cheese...it's time to get serious.

There's no reason we all shouldn't be red carpet-ready, with trim waists, flat abs and Michelle Obama arms. A life of mid-riff baring and tank top wearing is about to begin! Stick with me, follow the program outlined in this book, and you're on your way.

Let's Bust Some Exercise Myths!

There are a lot of misconceptions
about exercise that I want to address.
Over 25 years of experience
and working with clients have provided
me with an amazing laboratory to watch
how exercise really works.
Here are a few things I've learned:

COMMON MYTHS

MYTH #1

I'M DOING SO MUCH EXERCISE AND IT'S NOT WORKING!

More crunches do not necessarily make flat abs. If some are good, more are not necessarily better. I've spent a long time figuring out an abs routine that targets the zillions of little muscles in your abdominal region: In this book, we're going to hit them all. And later, we're going to get to your diet, because unless you stop eating muffins you're going to be hiding all these gorgeous muscles under a muffin top.

MYTH #2

IF I STOP TRAINING, MY MUSCLES WILL TURN TO FAT!

Before we build muscle, we must reduce body fat. My programs are based on circuit training, which keeps your heartrate up, so not only are you going to shape and tone your muscles, you're going to melt away the unwanted fat that's covering up the muscles. And if you ever stop training, your body may get fat, but it won't be because you ever had muscles. You may become soft, but that's a different story...

MYTH #3

MYTH #4

SPOT REDUCTION IS IMPOSSIBLE

It's a tremendous myth that one cannot spot reduce. What I've realized over time is that you can hone in on any body part and with the proper amount of exercise shape and sculpt it. That's the basic principle behind these manuals, that you can edit the shape of your body, you can sculpt yourself. Can I make you three inches taller? No. but if you follow this guide, you can sculpt muscles you didn't even know you had and drastically change your appearance.

MY ARMS ARE GOING TO GET BULKY!

This is something I hear from my female clients, worried they'll come out bulky and unfeminine. The truth is: the female body is not made to bulk. Unless you're genetically unique, you don't have the testosterone for Rocky Balboa biceps. If you follow these exercises with the prescribed weights, you won't bulk, you'll get sleeker and leaner.

In order to best target your abs and your arms, I'm going to ask you to get a few pieces of simple equipment.

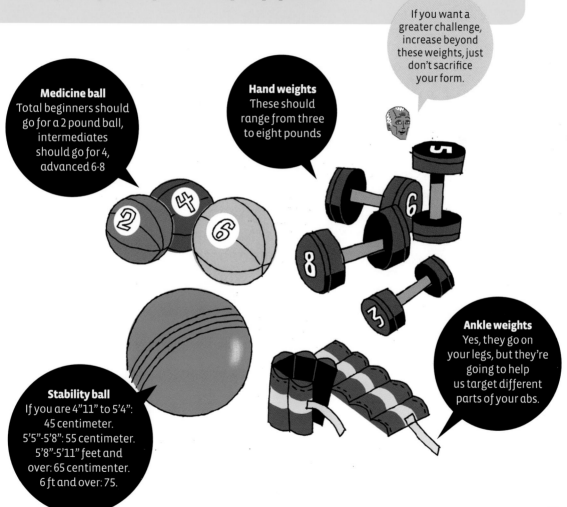

If you want a greater challenge, increase beyond these weights, just don't sacrifice your form.

Medicine ball
Total beginners should go for a 2 pound ball, intermediates should go for 4, advanced 6-8

Hand weights
These should range from three to eight pounds

Ankle weights
Yes, they go on your legs, but they're going to help us target different parts of your abs.

Stability ball
If you are 4"11" to 5'4": 45 centimeter.
5'5"-5'8": 55 centimeter.
5'8"-5'11" feet and over: 65 centimeter.
6 ft and over: 75.

ALTERNATIVE EQUIPMENT

I believe in integrating fitness into your life—you can't imagine the extra exercise I'm getting since having my twin daughters! Don't have handweights? Not a problem—grab two cans of beans or bottles of water and get to work.

I want you to look your best, I don't want you to get hurt. Stay focused when you're working out, and if you feel any pain, stop what you're doing right away. (Pain, by the way, is different than burn!) And if you're really, really in pain, please call your doctor.

This is a glossary. Use it like a Chinese menu. Pick two, three, four exercises depending on the time you've got. Do 15-20 repetitions each, two to three times minimum.

Now let's get started.

2

the
EXERCISES

ARMS

Strong arms make life easier. Whether you're carrying babies, groceries or your girlfriend's books to school, it's a wonderful feeling to be strong enough. And besides, toned arms look fantastic, on guys and on girls.

First, examine your body and set a realistic goal. For women with too much arm, you're going to increase your repetitions, increase the size of your circuit (pick at least four or five exercises each workout) and don't rest too much in between. You'll also need your cardio work to be intensive. Heavier weights will not get you to your goal any quicker. For women with scrawny arms: the pushup is king. Period.

For the guys out there, I'm guessing you're after bigger arms. Do as I do and start every day with 100-150 pushups. Take as long as you need, but set your number and get there. Start with five, or with ten, and in no time you'll be up to 25 a set. (And getting the added bonus of working your abs by keeping your core in check.)

❶

Start out in front of a mirror so you can check your alignment. Are your hands aligned properly? They should be directly under your shoulders and lined up with your chest. Make sure your core is nice and tight and your shoulders and neck are relaxed.

2

Visualize what you're trying to accomplish. You're going to use your triceps to help execute the perfect pushup, so make sure you feel them engage. Your body from shoulder to foot should be tight and even.

Focus on the contraction and isolate the muscle you want to work!

❶

Retract your shoulder blades and hold your elbows in at the sides. Keep your core tight, your knees soft.

2

Once everything is in the right position, simply contract your bicep. Don't let your shoulders rotate forward.

② SPIDERMAN PUSHUPS

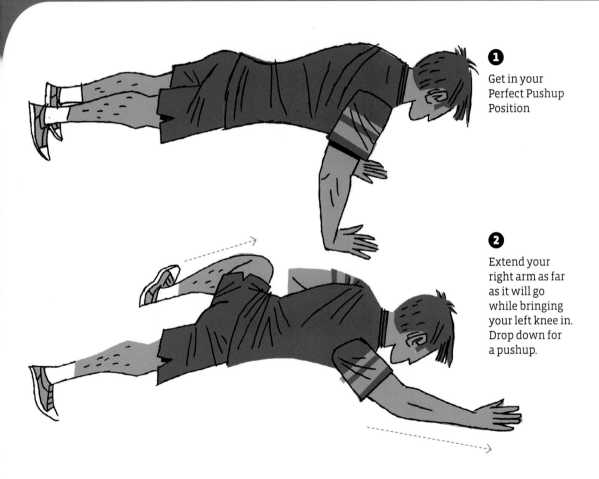

❶ Get in your Perfect Pushup Position

❷ Extend your right arm as far as it will go while bringing your left knee in. Drop down for a pushup.

3

Return to your PPP

4

Repeat on the opposite side

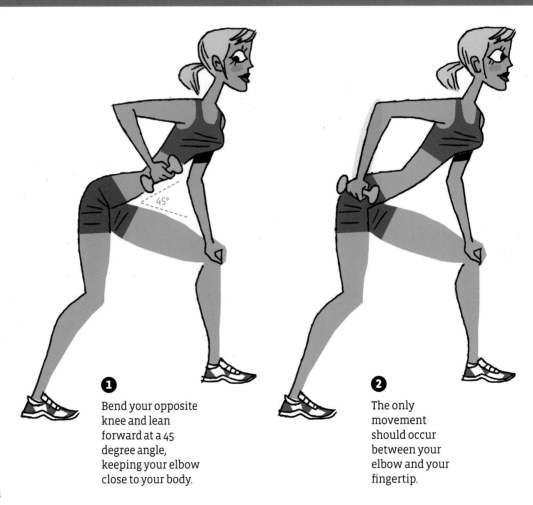

45°

❶ Bend your opposite knee and lean forward at a 45 degree angle, keeping your elbow close to your body.

❷ The only movement should occur between your elbow and your fingertip.

3 Fully contract your tricep.

For added burn, rotate your palm up as you extend your tricep.

② DIPS

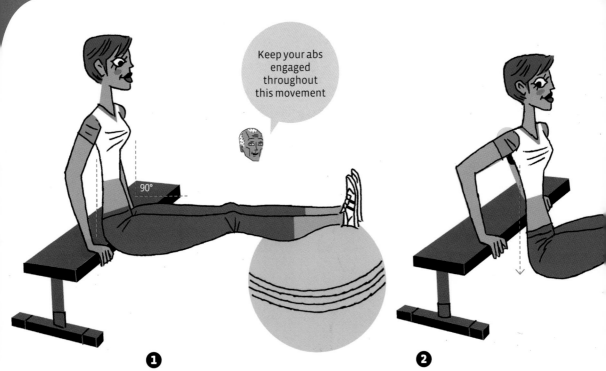

1 Keeping your back straight, extend your legs at a ninety degree angle to the top of your stability ball. Place the heels of your hand on the bend.

2 Keep your butt close to the bench and your shoulder blades back as you lower yourself down.

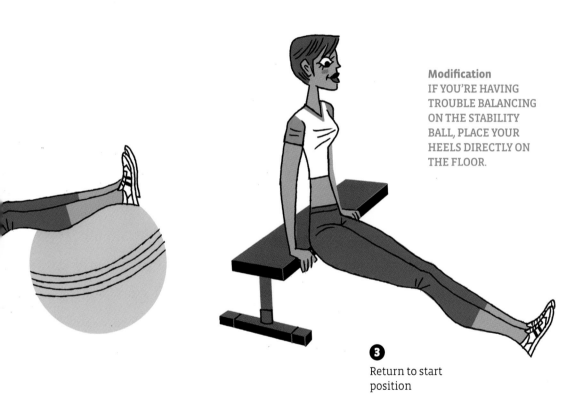

Modification
IF YOU'RE HAVING
TROUBLE BALANCING
ON THE STABILITY
BALL, PLACE YOUR
HEELS DIRECTLY ON
THE FLOOR.

❸
Return to start
position

② SHADOW BOXING

1

Stand with your feet shoulder-width apart, your knees soft and your core engaged. Punch across your body, fifteen reps on each side.

Add hand weights to pump up the intensity

90°

2 For upper cuts, start with your arm bent in a 90 degree angle. Punch upwards across your chest.

❶

Place your belly on a stability ball and your hands on the floor in front of the ball. Walk your hands forward until you are in a pushup position— Depending on your strength, your thighs, shins or toes should be on the ball. Whichever position you choose, don't let your hips sink!

❷

Adjust your palms so that your forefingers and thumbs touch one another, forming a diamond shape.

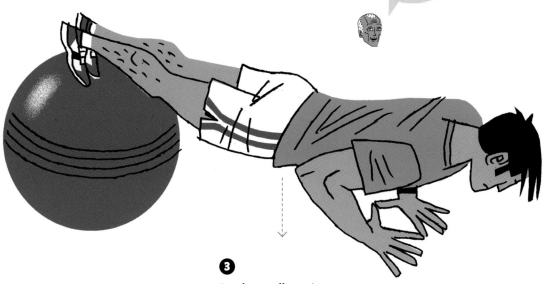

3

Bend your elbows in towards your sides as you lower to the floor. Exhale, and return to start position. Repeat 15 times.

❶

Get into perfect pushup position with the balls of your feet on the stability ball. Raise your hips toward the ceiling as you bring the ball towards your hands. Keep your abs tight, your legs straight and your balance should follow.

This is a very advanced move that will certainly get you lots of attention at the gym! But only try it if you're feeling strong and stable.

2

Once you're in a pike–or a "V" position, lower your torso down. Exhale, extend your elbows and return to the upward pike position. Repeat.

ABS

Is there any barometer for fitness like a gut? Whether you're a guy or a girl, you're always pinching that dreaded inch and sucking it in when you want to make a good impression. My goal for you is to let you exhale (ahhhh....) and still have a smooth, trim, flat set of abs.

All the crunches and planks in the world are not going to do anything if you're not following a sensible diet, so the first step to flat abs is watching what you eat. (There's a nutrition guide at the end of this book that spells it all out for you pretty clearly.)

After that, it's a question of repetition. Focus on your belly, on feeling the burn. Less can be more: fifteen perfect crunches are better than fifty sloppy ones. You'll know when you've got it right: you'll feel your muscles engage, you can almost feel the fat melting away. Whether your goal is size four jeans or enviable washboard abs, these are the moves that will get you there.

❶

Lie on a towel, or a mat, or even the floor with your knees at a 45 degree angle and your feet flat. Put your hands behind your head, with your fingers locked. Imagine there's a magnet in your belly button pulling your back down: do not arch your lower back!

2

Fix your eyes in a spot on the ceiling. Lift from your shoulders, not your neck. Contract, exhale at the top of the movement and inhale on the way back.

1

Place your hands on the floor, shoulder-width apart and positioned directly beneath your shoulders.

2

Keep your body straight. Resist the urge to stick your butt in the air!

3

HOLD! Start with 15 seconds at a time, and work your way up to a full minute.

Modification
PLACE YOUR FEET ON THE FLOOR, KEEPING YOUR BODY AS FLAT AS A BOARD.

❶
Lie flat on your back. Place one hand behind your head while crossing the opposite ankle over the opposite knee.

2

Fix your gaze on the ceiling and bring your elbow towards the raised knee.

3

Return slowly to start position.

1

Place your palms against the top of your stability ball.

The closer together you place your feet, the more challenging this exercise becomes.

2

Extend your legs and balance on the balls of your feet so that your body makes a 45 degree angle with the floor. Stretch through the crown of your head and reach through the back of your heels. Hold for 15 seconds at first, but work your way towards holding for a full minute.

❶

Place your palms on the foor, shoulder-width apart. Your feet should be resting atop your stability ball, your legs fully extended so that your body is parallel to the floor.

ABILITY BALL

❷

Pull the ball in towards your chest with a rolling motion. Hold for 15 seconds. Lower and repeat.

❶
Lie flat on your back. Spread your legs in as wide a "V" as possible.

Make sure to concentrate on lifting and squeezing your heels both IN and UP at the same time!

SORS

2
Press your hips into the floor as you exhale. Lift your flexed feet and squeeze them together in one, fluid motion. Continue to hold your heels together.

3
Inhale and lower your legs to the ground. Repeat.

Modification
IF YOU'RE FEELING STRONG, ADD ANKLE WEIGHTS.

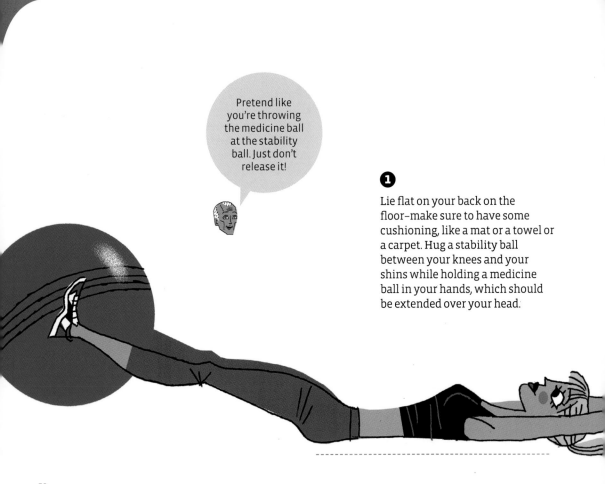

Pretend like you're throwing the medicine ball at the stability ball. Just don't release it!

❶

Lie flat on your back on the floor–make sure to have some cushioning, like a mat or a towel or a carpet. Hug a stability ball between your knees and your shins while holding a medicine ball in your hands, which should be extended over your head.

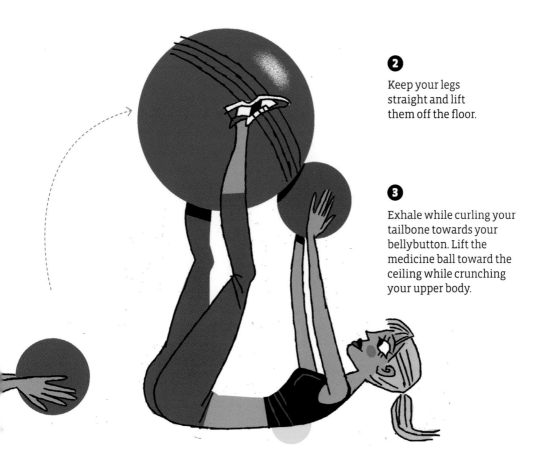

2

Keep your legs straight and lift them off the floor.

3

Exhale while curling your tailbone towards your bellybutton. Lift the medicine ball toward the ceiling while crunching your upper body.

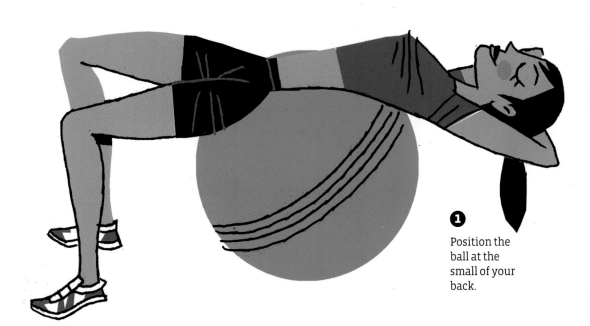

1

Position the ball at the small of your back.

ILITY BALL

The instability of the ball will work what Bridget Jones called "the wobbly bits."

❷

Fix your gaze at a point above your head. Exhale and lift your left elbow up towards your right knee. Inhale, lower and repeat.

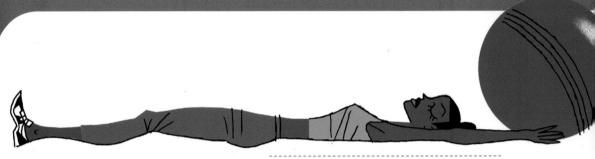

❶

Lie flat on your back, gripping your stability ball on both sides.

❷

Reach your arms and your legs straight up simultaneously.

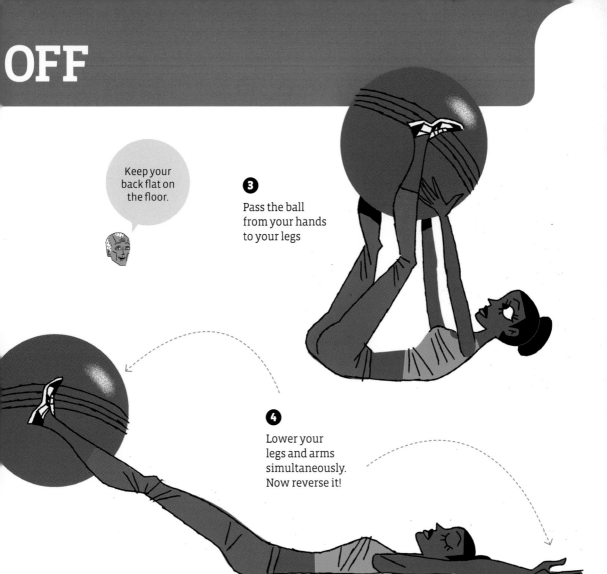

Keep your back flat on the floor.

3 Pass the ball from your hands to your legs

4 Lower your legs and arms simultaneously. Now reverse it!

57

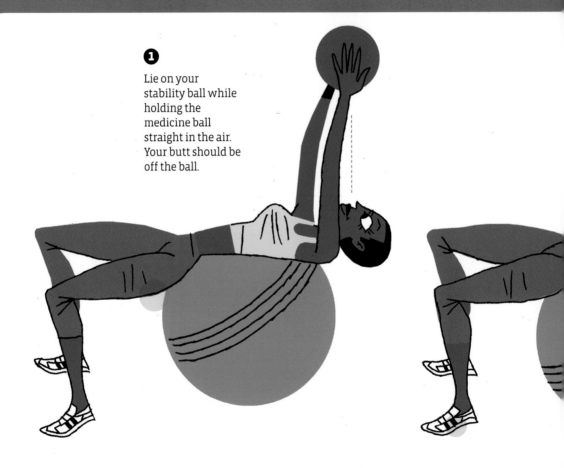

1

Lie on your stability ball while holding the medicine ball straight in the air. Your butt should be off the ball.

2

Keep your arms straight and rotate your upper body to the side. Your feet should remain flat on the floor.

3

Reverse. Remember that your waist is the fulcrum of the motion.

The closer together you place your feet, the more challenging this exercise will be

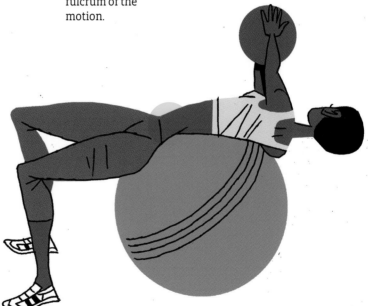

3

CIRCUIT
TRAINING

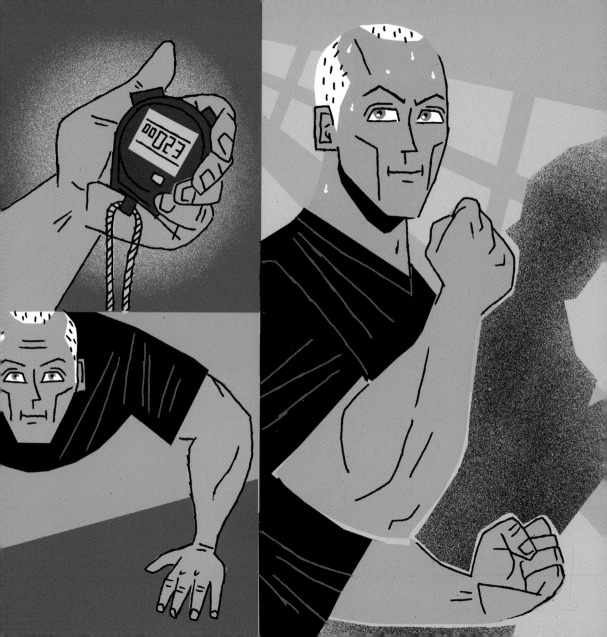

Circuit training is a way of getting the maximum effect of your exercises by combining strength and flexibility in a series of complementary moves done one after another without respite. I love it! It's an incredibly efficient way to tone and burn calories at the very same time. You're going to work your upper and lower bodies and you're going to work up a sweat. This isn't for the beginner, this isn't for the weak. You might even hate me for a minute or two, but you're going to love the result.

❶

SQUAT THRUST
Start with 15—but I'll always take more.

❷

MOUNTAIN CLIMBERS
Start out with 30 seconds, and increase to a minute as you get stronger

3

SHADOW BOXING
Upper cuts and
cross overs. Go
for 30 seconds on
each side

③ CIRCUIT #2

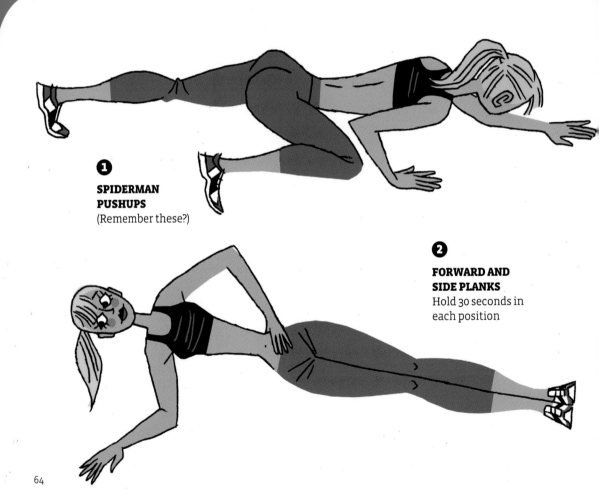

❶
**SPIDERMAN
PUSHUPS**
(Remember these?)

❷
**FORWARD AND
SIDE PLANKS**
Hold 30 seconds in
each position

3

DOUBLE CRUNCHES

You did these by handing a stability ball back and forth before. Now keep the stability ball between your ankles and add a medicine ball to your hands.

4
CARDIO

All of the pushups, dumbbell curls and crunches in the world won't mean a thing if you're not getting in a few solid cardio workouts every week. Think of it like baking a cake, and then forgetting to put the icing on top. (Not, by the way, that you should be eating cake and icing while you're on the plan. Unless it's your birthday; if it's your birthday, eat some cake!)

It's very important to figure out a cardio plan that works with your life, because you're going to need to stick with it.

Before you even think about working out, think about all of the ways you can move around a bit more in your daily life. If you have the choice between an elevator and a flight of stairs, choose the stairs. Park a little bit further away from your destination and hoof the extra blocks.

If you have access to a gym, that's terrific. On the following page, you'll see some prescriptions for gym-based cardio workouts that will help you lose the fat that might be hiding your sexy new arms and your awesome six pack. In my opinion, the best cardio machines for toning and sculpting your abs and arms are the rowing machine, the upper body ergometer and versaclimber. Take an honest assessment of your fitness level, and when any workout gets easy, I want you to switch it up: crank the machine to a higher level, stay on it ten minutes more. (Sitting on the equipment doesn't do anything, by the way.) I can't tell you how many people I've seen chatting away at the gym, reading magazines and never breaking a sweat and then wondering why they haven't seen the benefits of their "trips to the gym."

If you don't belong to a gym, that's no excuse for not getting in some solid cardio workouts. My friend Amy swears by her 45 minute jump rope class, and judging from how rocking her body is looking, I would say she's right! A jump rope is cheap, it's portable, and you can do it anywhere. Just crank up the music and jump like you did when you were a kid—if you keep tripping on the rope, just keep practicing. You'll be amazed at how quickly you'll pick it up.

Tennis is another great sport, and if you have any question about the power of swimming, just take a look at Dara Torres and Michael Phelps. Need I say more? Play a game of pickup basketball or soccer, go for a jog when the weather gets nice. Sign up for your local running club—set the goal of doing a 5K if that will help you get motivated. Races can also have the fantastic fringe benefit of raising money for local charities, as a lot of them sponsor races. I do a run for God's Love We Deliver every year, and knowing that my running that race is doing good for other people is a tremendous motivation. Get on line and find a cause that matters to you and see if they've got a walk, a run, a race and stick to it. Find a walking partner if you like company—but know that you should probably be too out of breath for a really good gossip.

If I'm being totally honest, I'll confess that I don't love doing my cardio workout on the machines at the gym. I like to head outside for a long bike ride in Central Park, or push my twin daughters' stroller around the city while walking at a reasonably fast clip. And I really love boxing—it's a really phenomenal workout. (Not to mention a great way to release stress!) I once turned up at a local boxing gym for an hour of sparring, jumping rope and circuit training. I thought I was so fit that class would be a breeze. Wrong! After twenty minutes, I felt like I was

SAMPLE CARDIO WORKOUTS:

1. 2500 meters on the rowing machine (Get it done as quickly as you can!)
2. 15 minutes on the Versa Climber
3. 15 minutes on the Upper Body Ergometer

ONCE YOU'VE MASTERED THAT, STEP IT UP:

1. 5000 meters on the rowing machine
2. 30 minutes on the Versa Climber
3. 10 minutes on the Upper Body Ergometer.

wearing cement slippers!

So get out there and find something you enjoy. Get a real sweat on—a real, dripping, pink-cheeked sweat—and keep at it. It's terrific for your skin, it's amazing for your heart, and it's an all-important piece in getting the abs and arms of your dreams.

MPRE is MAXIMUM PERCEIVED RATE OF EXERTION.

MPRE is a subjective gauge of how hard you're pushing yourself. Sure, there are devices and gadgets that tell you how hard you're working, but I'm going to ask you to gauge yourself, on a scale from one to ten. Here are the questions to ask yourself:

1. *Am I sweating?*
2. *Do I feel my heart rate increasing?*
3. *Could I maintain a conversation during this workout?*
4. *Am I feeling a muscle burn?*

When you're first starting out, allow yourself a little latitude.

As you get more exercise proficient, turn that dial up. It's when you start pushing your limits that you'll see great results.

You need to reach inside yourself. You're setting your internal speedometer, you know when you're reaching your own personal red zone.

DON'T

To those of you that load up for your cardio session with PDA's, magazines, and the latest gossip rag—you know who you are— take note. As I say with my workouts, make them mindful and make them efficient and effective. The same is true for cardio.

I want you to sweat. I want you to feel your butt engaged. I want you to feel every day that you're pushing yourself to the limit and beyond. No less will do if you're after the perfect body.

5
FOOD

Dairy
With all due respect to Elsie the cow, I don't suggest a large portion of dairy before putting on a string bikini.

Bread
For really flat abs, the bread's gotta go.

Excess fruit
Fruit is sugar, sugar gives you bloat.

Sweets!
Do I even need to tell you this? Don't eat them! No cookies, no chips

Certain foods puff you up, and if your goal is flat abs, you'll want to avoid them.

DO!
Eat a simple salad with a light vinagrette and a clean, grilled protein on top and you'll be bouncing quarters off your belly button.

Poultry
The butt man likes a skinless breast.

Fish
Small cold water fish like salmon and sardines are best.

Greens
Broccoli, spinach, and asparagus are the dieting MVP.

Fruit
Berries are the bomb.

THE MEAL PLAN

I believe in five small meals a day, so you should plan on eating something every three hours. I can't overemphasize the importance of breakfast. I'd like you to consume the bulk of your calories and carbohydrates before 2 pm. Also, please stick to my healthy snack

and 3 hours later...

start...

7:00 am
Good morning! Grab some protein in the form of a shake or some egg whites.

10:00 am
Protein again! Whichever you didn't have for breakfast you should have as a mid-morning snack.

options! And don't be too hard on yourself. There may be some potholes along the road to your flat abs, but don't despair. It's happened to the best bodies out there. Remember to stay the course, and just sweat a little bit harder the next day.

snack time...

finish!

1:00 pm
Take a power lunch: choose a lean protein (chicken, turkey, tuna) and mix it with some greens. You can also choose a healthy, starchy grain at lunch time: a slice of whole grain bread, a cup of steamed brown rice.

4:00 pm
Snack on a protein: a handful of almonds is always a good choice.

7:00 pm
For dinner, go for the same idea as lunch: lean protein, green vegetables, but this time, skip the starchy carb.

AT HOME

Get any and all food demons right out of your house. Can't resist cookies and chips? Don't buy them! Your home should be the safest place for keeping to your new-body meal plan, stocked with lean proteins and healthy vegetables and grains.

AT THE OFFICE

Use half of your lunchtime for a power walk around the block. Crummy weather? A series of squats at your desk can only help....

STICKING TO IT

I've been known to take my clients out to eat in order to teach them how best to navigate a menu. It is possible! Call the restaurant ahead of time (or check on-line) to look at the menu. It's easier to make sensible choices in advance. Then banish bread, and stick to the smart choice you made before you got hungry.

I'm no sadist. Enjoy yourself! Put an umbrella in that drink (please, please limit it to one!!), kick back, and rock that new bikini. You've earned it!

If you've followed the exercises and cardio tips in this book, you should start feeling more confident about baring those sexy arms and abs. I want you to go out and do one thing you wouldn't do before you got fit: spend a day in a bikini at the beach, rock a pair of low-riding jeans, buy your t-shirts a size smaller than you used to. Now stop walking and strut. You've earned it.